THE JOINT PROPERTY TAX TRAP

The Perils and Pitfalls of Joint Property and Real Planning Solutions

Jeffrey G. Marsocci, Esq.

Domestic Partner Publishing, LLC

The Joint Property Tax Trap

The Perils and Pitfalls of Joint Property and Real Planning Solutions

Note regarding legal counsel

As with any product, it is important to be clear about its intended purpose and use to avoid any misunderstandings. Specifically with writings about legal issues, it is noted that these materials are not a substitute for competent legal counsel. The contents of this book are instead written to provide information about common estate planning problems faced by domestic partners, and it is designed for general educational purposes only. The contents of this book are not to be construed as legal advice, and no attorney-client privilege exists between the reader and the author and/or publisher. In addition, laws change frequently, and therefore you also are urged to speak with an attorney about changes in the law that may affect you.

Circular 230 Disclosure: To ensure compliance with requirements imposed by the Internal Revenue Service, unless specifically indicated otherwise, any tax advice contained in this communication (including any accompanying literature) was not intended or written to be used, and cannot be used, for the purpose of avoiding tax-related penalties or promoting, marketing, or recommending to another party any tax-related matter addressed herein. For specific legal advice, you are urged to contact an attorney in your state or jurisdiction.

Copyright 2010 Domestic Partner Publishing, LLC

The Perils and Pitfalls of Joint Property and Real Planning Solutions

About the Author

Jeffrey G. Marsocci was born in Fort Worth, Texas, and raised in Lincoln, Rhode Island, where he graduated from Mount Saint Charles Academy High School. He received his Bachelor's degree in Business Administration from Hofstra University in Hempstead, NY, and two years later earned his law degree from Hofstra University School of Law.

In 2004, he received a Certificate Degree in Non-Profit Management from Duke University, and has earned his Legal Master of Estate Preservation designation from the *Abts Institute for Estate Preservation* in the same year. Jeff also serves as a member of the Legal Council for The Estate Plan, a nationally recognized estate preservation company headed by Henry Abts, trust guru and author of *The Living Trust*.

Mr. Marsocci has led his own firm in Raleigh, North Carolina, since 1996, focusing on the areas of Wills, Trusts and Life & Estate Planning and Administration with a concentration on helping his clients plan ahead to avoid problems rather than clean them up afterwards. He is also a founding member of The National Institute for Domestic Partner Estate Planning, and he frequently participates in programs to educate attorneys, financial advisors and accountants on estate planning issues.

In addition to this book, Mr. Marsocci has also written *The Anti-Probate Revolution*, *Estate Planning for Domestic Partners*, and *Estate Planning for Married Couples*, all available online. Jeff and his wife Kathleen are active Kiwanis members, working with the college-based service organization Circle K throughout North Carolina and South Carolina. Jeff and Kathy also each received the President's Call to Service Award for performing more than 4,000 hours of service during their lifetimes.

The Perils and Pitfalls of Joint Property and Real Planning Solutions

The Perils and Pitfalls of Joint Property and Real Planning Solutions

This book is dedicated to people who take the time to learn. Things tend to work out better for them and their loved ones.

The Perils and Pitfalls of Joint Property and Real Planning Solutions

Table of Contents

Introduction		1
Chapter One	Goals That Lead to Joint Property	5
Chapter Two	The Insidious Gift Tax	13
Chapter Three	The Lost Tax Benefits of Inheritance	21
Chapter Four	Lawsuits	29
Chapter Five	Inheritance and Lifetime Solutions	35

Introduction

There are tremendous benefits available to people who plan ahead the right way, and huge tax and legal problems for those who act upon simple folk remedies. And nowhere is there more "folklore" than around retitling accounts as "joint with a right of survivorship." And it happens all of the time.

A widower walks into a bank, and his estate planning consists of putting his children's names on all of his accounts. A widow calls her financial advisor and wants to put her daughter's name on her accounts so she can have access to her money in an emergency. Joint property with a right of survivorship was fine for a married couple, so it should be absolutely fine to do the same thing with children or other loved ones. Isn't it?

No it isn't. And the folk remedy of joint property with a right of survivorship is running rampant throughout the financial and banking industry. The reason this folk remedy is perpetuated is because it actually works... but only for married couples.

When a couple gets married, they inevitably sit down, review their finances, and start to consolidate accounts and assets. The banks and other financial institutions close down individual checking accounts and create one account as joint with a right of survivorship. Then the married couple moves from renting an apartment to buying a house, and the house is then titled as joint with a right of survivorship. They begin to earn some money and start to invest, and the brokerage account or mutual fund is titled as joint with a right of survivorship.

Somewhere in all of these changes, someone who would consider themselves a financial professional probably told the couple that if one of them passed on then the other would automatically inherit everything without probate. They may have also interjected "well, that's what most married couples do" and so it is what they should do "just in case something happens."

And they were correct. And the extended, costly and intrusive court process of probate is *certainly* something to be avoided, even for married couples. However, the impression on the couple is not "this is a great thing for married couples to do to avoid a lot of problems." The lasting impression seems to be "this is a great thing for *anyone at all* to do to avoid a lot of problems."

Years later, perhaps one member of the married couple did pass on, or became sick, or a friend or family member passed on, and comments are made like, "everything was joint with a right of survivorship, so there was no probate, *and it was so easy....*"

Suddenly, joint property with a right of survivorship becomes the estate planning technique of choice because it is so simple, inexpensive, and, best of all, you don't need a lawyer to make use of it. "Wow, this is fantastic! Everyone should do this!"

And so now that Mom is a widow or Dad is a widower and they want to make sure their estate passes on just as easily to the children, they decide (or the children suggest) that all of the parent's assets be retitled as " joint with a right of survivorship" with all of the children. And this is where all of the the trouble starts.

There are three severe drawbacks to titling assets as joint property with a right of survivorship, and hardly anyone outside of some financial professionals, some estate planning attorneys, and various people at the IRS and state department of revenue personnel. The problems are 1) state and federal gift taxes are imposed on the retitling of assets and accounts, 2) the stepped up basis on inherited property is lost for at least half of the property, and 3) lawsuit liability appears.

The potential for the family losing money to unnecessary taxes, a divorce for a child, and other lawsuits is substantial. And, unfortunately, many professionals are woefully ignorant of just how devastating mistakes in this area can be. For the professionals who are not well-versed in life and estate planning techniques, they end up counseling their clients to take the imprudent step of retitling ownership as joint with a right of survivorship. More often, they are unaware of the consequences and merely remain silent while filling out the paperwork as their clients request.

But there are solutions that do work to avoid probate. For now, please read on, and, more importantly, act upon what you read.

The Perils and Pitfalls of Joint Property and Real Planning Solutions

Chapter One:
Goals That Lead to Joint Property

"Mom, we have to do this," the middle aged woman said. "Things worked out fine when you and Dad did it, so it will work just as well if you put our names on your accounts and the deed for the house. We need to make sure you are protected."

Her mother looked back at her daughter across the dining room table, taking a sip from her tea. "I know you've talked about this to me, but you don't seem to be listening to me," Mom said. "You talked to your banker friend Connie, but my friend Mildred actually talked to an attorney who knows about this stuff. I have an appointment with the same attorney next week."

"But Mom," she pleaded. "What if you get sick? What if you pass on? Uncle Johnny didn't have joint property with a right of survivorship on the account with his children, and everything had to go through the probate court. It took two years for everything to get done. And he was sick for six months and the bills just kept piling up. All the attorney is going to do is tell you to put everything in our names as joint with a right of survivorship anyway, and you'll have to pay them to tell you that."

"Oh, so you're an attorney now, are you?" Mom asked. "Mildred told me that her attorney warned her that joint property would trigger some pretty big taxes and leave things open to lawsuits. She said her attorney is working on a better way to do things without taxes and lawsuits. You'll forgive me if I trust Mildred's attorney more than Connie who was a bank teller ten years ago. It's still my money, dear, and I'm going to meet with the attorney to see what they have to say. I can always go to the bank later and handle the paperwork, but you'll pardon me if I do things the way I want to."

The daughter sat back, shaking her head. What she didn't realize is that Mom's wisdom and patience that day saved the family a lot of money in taxes and from her sister's divorcing husband the next year. Had she in fact retitled her accounts and home as joint with a right of survivorship, there would have been substantial tax, financial, and lawsuit liability problems. But there were better ways to reach the family's planning goals, and Mom was already pursuing them despite her daughter's so-called "legal" information.

This happens every day in banks and credit unions across the country. It happens every day in real estate and mortgage offices with deeds, and in brokerage houses and financial advisor offices with stock accounts and mutual funds, and even in attorney's conference rooms throughout the country. The quick, easy, and inexpensive folk remedy to planning ills seems to be "joint property with a right of survivorship." However, with the exception of married couples, this can be one of the biggest planning mistakes a person can make.

By why are people going to the bank to have their accounts redone? Because joint property with a right of survivorship does address two main planning goals, particularly for widows and widowers. Unfortunately, there are some pretty hefty tax and liability problems that go along with it, and there are more effective solutions. For this chapter, we will outline the planning goals that usually lead people to erroneously change their accounts and assets.

Avoidance of Probate

By far, the most compelling reason people choose to retitle their accounts with their children or other loved ones is to avoid the probate court process upon death. By having "joint property with a right of survivorship" with the chosen beneficiaries, the assets pass to the survivors without probate and all of its inherent costs, delays, and loss of privacy.

Despite protests from attorneys who claim "probate fees aren't that bad in our state," the fact is that according to an AARP study probate claims between four and ten percent (4%-10%) of an estate, takes six months to a year and a half to complete the probate court process, and all financial information submitted to the court is open to public scrutiny. No one wants to go through that process, but unless steps are taken to avoid probate, then it will happen.

With joint property with a right of survivorship, when a person passes on, their share is automatically inherited by the other joint owners without probate. However, there are some inheritance drawbacks in addition to the tax problems discussed later in the book.

First, the other joint owners inherit the asset right away. While this may be what most people want if they have responsible adult children, others may have placed age or other restrictions on inheritance within their Will. These restrictions do not apply to assets inherited through a right of survivorship. For example, if a child is 25 and you decide an appropriate age to inherit assets is 40, then the asset would be inherited right away. (In point of fact, the asset is actually owned with the 25 year old child right away).

Second, there are no provisions in joint property with a right of survivorship for children of the joint owners. Most people wish for their children to inherit their property, but if that child passes on first, most people want their grandchildren to receive that share. With joint property, the assets simply bypass the grandchildren and go automatically to the other joint owners.

Finally, there are no restrictions on what the money can be used for. If a person wishes to name a grandchild as the joint owner with a right of survivorship, but they want the account to be used for college or other advanced education, then there is nothing that says the child has to use it for those purposes. They could go out and spend the money on a sports car or a vacation to Las Vegas if they wish.

For inheritance purposes, joint property with a right of survivorship does allow the other joint owners to bypass the probate court process, but no restrictions can be placed on how and when the asset is inherited.

Access and Control

While automatic inheritance usually tops the goals for using joint property with a right of survivorship, the second most prevalent reason is to allow a loved one to have access to accounts should you fall ill. This is certainly a worthy goal, but there are some deficiencies in this as well.

First, access and control is given right away to the other owners. It does not matter if you intend to only allow the other joint owners access if you become ill; they have access right away.

The second point, which is related to the first, is that the money from the accounts can be taken out by the other joint owners right away and used for themselves. There are no safeguards that say the accounts only have to be used for the person they belonged to before the change. So Mom may wish for her children to have access to her checking and investment accounts to pay for her bills if she becomes sick and can not handle things on her own anymore, but her son could take the money out now and spend the money on a big vacation. And there is nothing Mom can do about it.

Third, because there are no safeguards on this money, it could create substantial problems within the family if the parent only listed one child as the joint owner. Suddenly, every expenditure paid and every penny taken out is scrutinized by the other children, and family discord is a distinct possibility.

Summary

There are two main reasons that people consider using joint property with a right of survivorship—control during a period of illness and inheritance upon death. However, joint property with a right of survivorship carries some substantial drawbacks and problems which we will cover in the following chapters.

Chapter Two:
The Insidious Gift Tax

"It's my money, and I'll do whatever I want with it!!"

James was doing his best to help his client, but if Mr. Branco did not want to listen, then there was nothing he could do. And with Mr. Branco being 83, he thought he had seen it all. "Of course you can," James said. "But there are tax consequences to changing all of your bank and investment accounts to joint property with a right of survivorship. There is something called a federal gift tax, and you can only give so much money to your son each year."

"But I'm not giving it to him," Mr. Branco interrupted. "I'm only putting his name on my account."

"Yes, but it's the same thing in the eyes of the law," James replied. "Tax-wise, putting your son's name on everything is the same as if you were giving him half of everything, and you should tell your accountant about this before you make any changes so he can advise you about taxes."

"No, he's just going to make a big deal out of nothing," Mr. Branco said. "Look, you're my financial advisor, so just make the changes."

"OK, you're the boss," James said. *Then he pulled out a piece of paper from his desk drawer.* "Please sign this form saying that we told you about the *potential tax consequences of retitling your accounts and I'll get the other paperwork started."*

About three years later, after Mr. Branco passed on, his accountant called James, furious over the hundreds of thousands of dollars in taxes, interest and penalties that had to be paid because of the account changes. James calmly responded by offering to fax a copy of the signed form to his office.

In every year, each person is only allowed to give another person a certain amount (in 2009 up to $13,000) without any federal gift taxes. After that, the IRS imposes a gift tax on the giver of the money. So if Parent A gives Child B $30,000 in cash, $17,000 is subject to federal gift taxes. The same thing is true when a parent takes all of their individual property and assets and "puts their child's name" on the title. The effect is that half of the fair market value of all of these assets that exceed $13,000 is considered a gift to the child.

While many bankers, attorneys, and even some accountants do not counsel their clients on gift taxes, the tax is very real. However, in many cases you do not have to actually *pay* any federal gift taxes, but the $17,000 is *subject* to gift taxes… it is just that Uncle Sam has graciously given you an additional lifetime bank of $1,000,000 to draw against before, as the giver, you have to *pay* federal gift taxes tax money out of your pocket when you give a gift. That's the good news. The bad news is that every dollar you draw against is decreasing the amount you are allowed to give away upon death without estate taxes. (The 2009 federal estate tax exemption is $3,500,000, and in 2011 drops to $1,000,000.)

I also want to be extremely clear in how the gift tax works. In 2009, only $13,000 can be gifted each year from a parent to a child, and anyone else for that matter, except for married couples. They can give as much as they want, back and forth, as often as they want. But anyone can give *as many* $13,000 gifts away as they want as long as it is to *different* people. So in one year a Parent can give $13,000 in gifts to their child Benny, their nephew Clyde, their niece Darlene, their friend Evan, and their sister Flo. That's $65,000 in gifts, but there are no gift tax implications because no more than $13,000 went to any one person. While this can be considered a bit of a benefit, it does not usually help families since they want to plan for inheritance with their children and not the world at large.

THE JOINT PROPERTY TAX TRAP

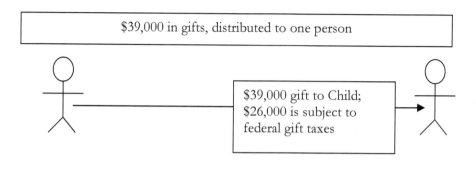

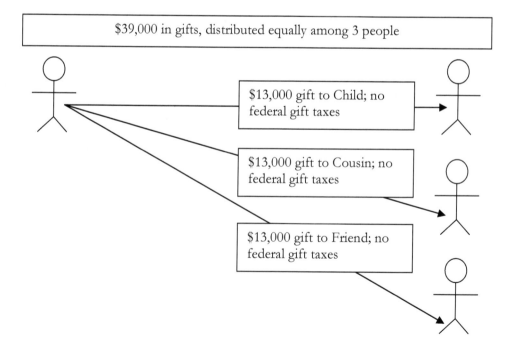

The Perils and Pitfalls of Joint Property and Real Planning Solutions

Confused still? Here's an example that illustrates both the gift tax and estate tax problem of using joint property:

> In 2011, Carlos and his son Dave are planning for Carlos' estate and possible incapacity, and, based on the advice they got from their cable guy Larry, decide to put all of Carlos' assets into joint property with a right of survivorship. This means that all of Carlos' previously separate accounts now have the son Dave listed as an owner. Carlos only has a house worth $600,000 and a brokerage account worth $400,000. After they put Dave's name on the title to the house and the brokerage account, they decide to talk to their accountant.
>
> The accountant gave them the bad news that Carlos actually gave a gift of $500,000 to Dave, the first $13,000 of which is exempt, leaving a taxable gift of $487,000 from Carlos to his son Dave. Assuming Carlos started with the whole $1,000,000 in lifetime tax credits, we subtract the $487,000 from the $1,000,000 leaving $563,000 that can be gifted in the future (beyond the $13,000 annual exclusion), OR only $563,000 that can passed from Carlos to Dave, or anyone else for that matter, without estate taxes.

For many people, that may not sound so terrible, but imagine if Carlos did not go to his accountant and fill out the proper gift tax forms. That's when you usually hear two of the IRS' favorite words—"interest" and "penalties." There is also a huge potential *state* gift tax problem, depending on the state you reside in. For example, in North Carolina prior to 2009 this would have actually resulted in an immediate tax of $19,430 due from Carlos for his gifts to his son Dave.

A total of $19,430 in taxes would have to be paid, out of pocket and right away, as a result of retitling these two assets as joint with a right of survivorship. (I wonder if the cable guy Larry has legal malpractice insurance?)

All of this came about because Carlos wanted to provide for his son Dave should he pass on and to allow Dave to take over management of his assets if he becomes incapable of handling things himself. This simply does not sound "right" to a lot of people since they believe that in America they are able to give their property to anyone they choose without being taxed, but I can assure you that this tax is very real. And, no, this tax does not affect married couples at all because they have something called the "unlimited marital deduction," which allows unlimited gifts and unlimited inheritance without taxes for U.S. Citizen spouses. For Carlos, it is probably because his experience with his wife prior to her passing on was that joint property was an extremely easy way of settling things, and it is possible that if his wife became incapacitated that Carlos simply kept managing the joint accounts without interruption. But things are much different outside of the husband-wife relationship.

As an added note, retitling assets as joint property with a right of survivorship with one child with the intent of having that child redistribute everything fairly to their siblings is an even worse idea. At the point of inheritance, you are now saddling the responsible child with the moral obligation to distribute assets to their siblings as soon as possible but they now also have the same gift tax obligations if they "give" more than $13,000 in a given year to a sibling.

Summary

While joint property with a right of survivorship provides easy inheritance and control in case of illness, it comes with some potentially large gift tax consequences. Before making changes to the ownership of any account, please first contact a financial or tax professional familiar with the gift tax.

The Perils and Pitfalls of Joint Property and Real Planning Solutions

Chapter Three:
The Lost Tax Benefits of Inheritance

"Gosh, it was so easy," Tom, the oldest son, told his mother's accountant. "Mom had put everything into all of our names as joint property with a right of survivorship and her estate completely avoided probate. It was very easy to sell everything off and divide the cash three ways."

Their accountant Damon looked at them trying not to show the chill that just ran through him. "When did your mother make the changes to her accounts? She never told me."

"Oh, it has to be about five years ago," Shelly, the middle child said while smiling. "That's not a problem, is it?"

Damon sat back in his chair, frowning. "Actually, it is a problem," he said. "A pretty big one. Unless your mother used another accountant to fill out the gift tax forms. But even then, the bigger problem is you just sold everything."

"But that's what Mom wanted," Charlie, the youngest child, said. "She told us to go and sell everything, so that's what we did."

"The problem is that there are some pretty steep capital gains taxes that you have to pay," Damon said, looking through some papers. "Your mother had a lot of stocks that she held on to for many years, and they all grew in value

from next to nothing to more than $1.5 million. The house was also worth a lot of money, and it had grown in value a lot in the 30 years since she bought it."

The children were now paying close attention, the smiles fading from their faces. "You're familiar with capital gains taxes," Damon said matter of factly. "According to the numbers I have, she had about $2,300,000 in assets when she died. However, her total tax basis was only $250,000. When someone dies, their tax basis is ratcheted up to the value on the date of death. However, when your mother put your names on everything she owned, she actually gave away three quarters of everything she owned to you along with her tax basis."

Damon then pulled out a calculator and started banging out numbers, the children watching intently. "According to this, because your mother gifted you three quarters of her assets along with her tax basis, $1,537,500 is subject to capital gains taxes," he said. He entered a few more numbers. "Unfortunately, when you sold everything you incurred capital gains taxes on those assets. We're looking at roughly $307,000 in taxes that are due."

"Wait a minute," Tom said, cutting off Damon's next point. "What are you talking about? Mom didn't have a taxable estate. She was below the $3.5 million mark. I don't understand."

Damon patiently continued, "Its not federal estate taxes that are due," he said. "It's capital gains taxes on the property, stocks, and other investments you were partially gifted years ago and then recently sold. If instead of being given those assets when your mother changed the ownership on the accounts she let you simply inherit them, then there would not have been any capital gains taxes at all."

Now it was the children's turn to feel shocked. They simply looked at each other. "No one ever told us," Charlie said. "We had no idea."

The Perils and Pitfalls of Joint Property and Real Planning Solutions

"I'm sorry, but your Mom never told me what she was doing," Damon said. "If I had known ahead of time, I could have warned her. Now all I can do is help accurately report the taxes."

Drawbacks of joint property with a right of survivorship don't end with the gift tax. In addition to the gift tax being imposed on the portion of the assets being retitled in the children's names, there is also a tax break being lost by using joint property with a right of survivorship. When someone passes on and their heirs inherit their assets, they get the assets at fair market value. It is then examined for estate taxes, and if any are due, they are paid. But then all assets can be sold at the date of death fair market value without any capital gains taxes. This "ratcheting up" of asset values is called a stepped-up basis. If assets are gifted away during life, then they do not receive the stepped up basis. Let's use a simple example of a stock account with Carlos and his son Dave:

Carlos has a $400,000 stock account and wishes to retitle the account as joint with a right of survivorship with his son Dave to avoid probate and allow Dave to access the account if he should fall ill. When Carlos originally invested in the stock, he put $100,000 into the account. Putting aside the gift tax implications and assuming there were no sales of stock during Carlos' life, when Carlos passes on his son Dave inherits the other half of the account valued on the date of death at $500,000. Dave then turns around and sells the stock for $500,000. Here is how the capital gains taxes are computed:

Steps

1) Carlos' original tax basis in the stock: $100,000 (what he paid for it)

2) Carlos retitles the account so now he owns half and Dave owns half

3) The tax basis in the property is now $50,000 for Carlos and $50,000 for Dave

4) Carlos' tax basis at Carlos death is $250,000 and Dave's tax basis at Carlos' death is $50,000

5) Sale of Stock is at $500,000 and the tax basis is at $300,000 (Carlos $250k + Dave $50k)

6) There is a $200,000 taxable gain

7) Capital Gains tax rate is 20%

8) Dave has to pay $50,000 in capital gains taxes

If Dave had simply inherited the stock account in full through a will or Revocable Living Trust rather than receiving the second half through joint tenancy with a right of survivorship, then he would not have to pay *any* capital gains taxes for this transaction.

While planning for incapacity and a smooth inheritance are legitimate goals, joint property is not the answer. There are solutions that allow a child or children to control their parent's assets if they fell ill and also to provide inheritance without probate, and those solutions are revocable living trusts, powers of attorney, and transfer upon death provisions.

The Perils and Pitfalls of Joint Property and Real Planning Solutions

To keep things brief, a revocable living trust is a document set up during a person's life that allows them to retitle their property into the name of the trust and still remain in control of everything because they are the trustee. For a couple, they create a joint trust where both of them are trustees. (Please note that having a last will and testament does not bypass probate. If anyone ever told you that their estate will not have to go through probate because they have a Will, then they are mistaken.)

In the case of Carlos and his son Dave, Carlos can create his own revocable living trust, maintain complete control over his assets, and name Dave as the successor trustee and beneficiary. If Carlos falls ill, Dave can take over management of his father's trust. If Carlos passes on, Dave takes control of distributing his father's estate.

A durable general power of attorney can help a child, or anyone else you choose, manage your assets if you fall ill. If done correctly, the power of attorney will allow your agent access to bank accounts, stock accounts, retirement accounts, and any other asset including the equity in the home.

One important item to note is that the power of attorney does nothing for inheritance. The power of attorney ends upon the person's death, so please do not believe that your estate is covered because you gave someone a power of attorney.

Finally, for inheritance purposes many accounts allow a "transfer upon death" or "pay upon death" provision. Using these techniques avoid probate and avoid the capital gains taxes problems that come with joint property with a right of survivorship. These techniques do have some drawbacks that a revocable living trust can avoid, but it is far better than joint property with a right of survivorship.

Summary

Joint property with a right of survivorship has gift tax consequences, but it can also have some severe capital gains tax issues for the other joint owners upon death and the sale of the assets. The lost tax benefits and severe tax consequences often far outweigh the administrative benefits of joint property, particularly because there are other options.

The Perils and Pitfalls of Joint Property and Real Planning Solutions

Chapter Four:
Lawsuits

"This is a nightmare," Donny said to his daughter's attorney. "I did not sign up for this, and I don't understand why I'm even here."

"I'm sorry you feel that way, and I can certainly understand it," Mary the attorney said. "But we have to deal with things the way they are now. The court has made it very clear that we don't have a choice."

Donny's daughter Victoria married badly. Her husband Rick had little ambition, and when he was laid off from work he decided to use his free time chasing younger women instead of finding a job. Now that Victoria caught Rick cheating after promises he would change his ways, she finally filed for divorce. The problem in front of them now is that Donny, a widower of several years, had changed all of his accounts and assets as joint with a right of survivorship with Victoria to make things easy in case he fell ill or passed on. And Rick wanted half.

"What does my daughter's sad excuse for a husband have to do with my house, my stock account, my checking and savings accounts, and just about everything else I own?" Donny asked. "I didn't marry him."

"Unfortunately, you technically and legally gave half of all of those things to your daughter when you retitled your house and accounts as joint with a right of survivorship," Mary said, motioning to the silent Victoria sitting across the desk from her. *"Because your daughter owns half of those assets, we have to comply with the court's order to add that half to the marital assets being split up."*

"And just what is the court going to do to me if I refuse to go along with this?" Donny asked. *"Arrest me? Take my house away and sell it?"*

"Yes," Mary said. *"They will."*

Donny looked stunned, and Victoria began to weep.

In addition to tax problems, there are also some legal complications that go along with joint property with a right of survivorship. These problems pop up for the same reasons that the taxes do—the person being added actually owns their share of the asset now and not at some point in the future when the other owner passes on. These legal complications can provide serious problems for the person putting their children or others on the account. These problems occur:

- During a divorce

- During a lawsuit

- If the child wants to "take the money and run."

Divorce

There is a fifty percent divorce rate in the United States. This means that there is a 1 in 2 chance that a marriage will end in divorce, which usually means a court battle will occur. During the divorce proceedings, assets need to be disclosed. As you read in the opening story for this chapter, those assets that are jointly owned with a parent become part of the assets that must be disclosed.

While each state has different rules and regulations on whether or not the assets will actually be split up with the divorcing spouse, there is a very good chance the assets at least have to be disclosed during the court processes.

"That's not fair! That's not right!" you may be saying. And you are correct. It is not right. But that is the way it is. By putting a child's name on an asset as joint with a right of survivorship, you are running the risk that those assets will be on the table for division during the divorce proceeding.

Lawsuits

Divorce is also not the only kind of lawsuit that can affect joint property held with another person. Any kind of lawsuit can also subject your assets to being lost in a legal action. If you retitle your assets as joint with a right of survivorship with your son and your son is in a car accident, has a business go under, or files for bankruptcy, then those assets could potentially be on the chopping block if your son loses.

The Perils and Pitfalls of Joint Property and Real Planning Solutions

There was a case in Florida where a woman put her daughter's name on her condominium as joint with a right of survivorship so that her daughter would automatically inherit her home if she passed on. Unfortunately, the daughter was involved in a bad car accident, it was the daughter's fault, and when she lost the lawsuit, the daughter declared bankruptcy because she couldn't pay such a huge judgment. The daughter got to keep her house. But Mom had to sell her house to help pay off the judgment.

Permanent Transfer

One possibility that parents almost never think about is their children taking advantage of the situation and taking the money. Unfortunately, this happens far too often.

If a parent retitles their bank account as joint with a right of survivorship with their child, the child now has access to the account as a joint owner. The child has access to the bank account and can take out as much money as they wish and there is nothing that says the child has to spend the money on their parent. If a parent retitles their home as joint property with a right of survivorship with their daughter, the child now owns half of the house. If the parent wants to sell the house, half of the proceeds are paid to the child and there is nothing saying the child has to give the parent the other half. In fact, the child may be able to block the sale of the house since they are an owner refusing to sell.

It is extremely easy for a parent to retitle their assets as joint with a right of survivorship with their child. It is another matter entirely to take the property back.

Summary

Joint property with a right of survivorship comes with large tax problems, but these may pale in comparison to the potential legal problems that may come along because of the joint owner. Losing the asset to divorce, bankruptcy, or other lawsuits are possible, and there is always the possibility that the joint owner can take the money and run. When that happens, it is not a large portion of the assets being lost to taxes... it's the entire asset being lost.

The Perils and Pitfalls of Joint Property and Real Planning Solutions

Chapter Five:
Inheritance and Lifetime Solutions

The middle-aged woman stood in the center of the bank floor screaming at the manager, her face distorted with rage and tears flowing down her cheeks, but the words coming through clear. "He's my father, he's in a coma, and you damn well better give me access to his money NOW!"

The people standing in line to make deposits took a step back, and one young woman with a toddler turned and walked out the door, gently nudging her child ahead of her while looking back.. "Ma'am, I've told you we can't do that..."

"You stupid moron, give me his MONEY!" she screamed. "I have to pay his bills or he'll lose the house, and I can't do that without access to his accounts!" If she saw the security guard walk up behind her with his hand on his taser, she didn't give any indication.

"We've already called the police," the manager said, trying to remain calm. "I know you are in a difficult position, but we told you to hire an attorney to help you get access to his accounts. Please leave now."

"How am I supposed to hire an attorney, idiot!" she yelled, turning to walk out the door. "I don't have the $5,000 the attorneys keep asking for. All of his money is in the accounts I can't get to!"

The Perils and Pitfalls of Joint Property and Real Planning Solutions

The Joint Property Tax Trap

Gail watched as the woman stormed out the door, trying unsuccessfully to slam the glass doors behind her. Gail then walked up to the bank manager. "Wow, are you OK?" she asked.

"I'll be fine," the manager said, rubbing his forehead. "I really feel bad for her, but I can't just open up a client's bank accounts to someone without the legal paperwork."

He straightened up, composing himself, and asked Gail, "What can I do for you?"

"Unfortunately, it looks like my mother is in the same kind of situation," Gail said. "But all of her accounts are owned by her living trust, and I'm her successor trustee. I was told you already have a copy of her trust on file and paperwork showing I'm the successor trustee, but here's the form from your bank that is signed by the doctors declaring her unable to handle her own financial affairs."

The manager took the form and looked it over, a slightly skeptical look coming over his face for a moment. But only a moment. "Here are the business cards of the doctors at the hospital," Gail said. "They said if there were any questions to call them."

"That's not necessary," the manager said. "I've worked with a few living trusts before, and it appears that everything is in order. Come with me, we'll pull up your father's file, and hopefully we can get you access to his accounts by this afternoon."

The Perils and Pitfalls of Joint Property and Real Planning Solutions

The Joint Property Tax Trap

Many families have laudable goals in wanting to change their assets to joint property with a right of survivorship. They wish to allow their loved ones to inherit their property without the rigors, expenses and delays of probate. They also wish to allow access to assets by a trusted friend or relative during a time of medical crisis or simply for convenience. However, the revocable living trust can do all of this without the tax, legal and financial problems that come along with joint property with a right of survivorship.

Inheritance

The Revocable Living Trust is quickly growing in popularity among middle class families of all demographics wishing to save their heirs time, taxes, and probate costs upon death. But, despite efforts to keep the existence of these trusts quiet by many in the legal profession, the revocable living trust is nothing new. The first recorded instances of trusts was circa 800 A.D. in the Roman Empire, and then adopted in the 12th Century in England to prevent the arbitrary confiscation of land by the crown. And speaking of revolutionary, the first recorded instance of a trust being used in the New World was created by a local attorney in Hanover County, Virginia in 1765. You may have heard of the attorney. His name was Patrick Henry. By no means is the revocable living trust a new entity.

These versatile trusts are today created during life and then upon death distribute property without probate court supervision or interference, and, most importantly for some, keeping the hands of probate attorneys out of their family's pockets. Instead, a less expensive, less time consuming process of settling a revocable living trust is used, and your successor trustee signs title to the assets over to the heirs.

For many people, this is the ideal method of inheritance because it avoids probate and it avoids the tax and other problems associated with joint property. However, it also addresses problems of potential sickness and incompetency during life.

Incapacity

Many people choose to look at joint tenancy with a right of survivorship as a way to allow a trusted loved one access to their finances should they fall ill. However, a revocable living trust can also provide assistance with this during a time of incapacity without the gift tax or legal and financial liability problems. In many cases, it is a simple matter of naming that trusted loved one as the "successor trustee" or even to act with you as a "joint trustee."

Simply put, a successor trustee can take over management of all trust assets in the event you become too ill to handle things yourself. At that time, a doctor can put in writing that you are unable to handle things yourself and then the successor trustee takes over. You may also realize that you may become incapacitated in the near future, and you can simply resign as trustee in writing and then the successor trustee can take over. In all cases, the terms of the trust must be reviewed to understand the incapacity process.

Another possibility is to name that trusted loved one as a joint trustee with you. This typically happens as people get older and they want a child to handle some financial matters for them now even if they are not incapacitated. In this case, a revocable living trust can be created for an individual with themselves and their child as equal co-trustees where either one of them can handle matters independently.

While the revocable living trust is available to handle both a smooth inheritance without probate court *and* to allow someone to handle financial matters on your behalf, some people are put off by the expenses involved in setting up a revocable living trust. If this is the case, then there may be other methods of avoiding probate upon inheritance such as beneficiary designations, but the proper method to give someone control of your financial assets during a time of incapacity is through a durable general power of attorney.

This "power of attorney" allows a person to handle your financial and legal matters during your life while you are incapacitated. However, it does not allow that person to deal with your assets after death. In legal terms, the power of attorney lets someone else legally handle certain matters just as if they were legally being done by you. Once you are legally deceased, you can not legally perform bank transactions, change the names on deeds, or handle stock trades, so a person can not use the power of attorney to do something you legally can not do.

Summary

There are solutions to help people plan ahead for inheritance or incapacity that do not have the tax, financial or legal drawbacks associated with joint property with a right of survivorship. A revocable living trust, beneficiary designations, and financial powers of attorney can help with different problems and potential problems. To make sure these items are addressed properly, please see an experienced life and estate planning attorney in your area.

In North Carolina, you can reach the author of this book who is also an attorney at:

The Law Offices of Jeffrey G. Marsocci, PLLC
8406 Six Forks Road, Suite 102
Raleigh, North Carolina 27615
(919) 844-7993
www.livingtrustlawfirm.com

If you do not know of an attorney in your area, Legis, Inc. is a company that provides trust and estate planning documents to attorneys, and they may be able to provide a reference for you. They can be reached at 1-888-875-1221. For additional reading materials on living trusts and other estate planning techniques, Mr. Marsocci's book *The Anti-Probate Revolution* can be purchased online, or for more detailed information, we also recommend *The Living Trust* by Henry W. Abts III, also available online and through bookstores everywhere.

Made in the USA
Columbia, SC
26 July 2022